HUMAN SERVICES (MEDICARE) ACT 1973 (AUSTRALIA)

2018 EDITION

Updated as of May 15, 2018

THE LAW LIBRARY

TABLE OF CONTENTS

Human Services (Medicare) Act 1973
No. 41, 1974
Compilation No. 45
Compilation date: 21 October 2016
Includes amendments up to: Act No. 61, 2016
Registered: 26 October 2016
About this compilation
This compilation
This is a compilation of the Human Services (Medicare) Act 1973 that shows the text of the law as amended and in force on 21 October 2016 (the compilation date).
The notes at the end of this compilation (the endnotes) include information about amending laws and the amendment history of provisions of the compiled law.
Uncommenced amendments
The effect of uncommenced amendments is not shown in the text of the compiled law. Any uncommenced amendments affecting the law are accessible on the Legislation Register (www.legislation.gov.au). The details of amendments made up to, but not commenced at, the compilation date are underlined in the endnotes. For more information on any uncommenced amendments, see the series page on the Legislation Register for the compiled law.
Application, saving and transitional provisions for provisions and amendments
If the operation of a provision or amendment of the compiled law is affected by an application, saving or transitional provision that is not included in this compilation, details are included in the endnotes.
Editorial changes
For more information about any editorial changes made in this compilation, see the endnotes.
Modifications
If the compiled law is modified by another law, the compiled law operates as modified but the modification does not amend the text of the law. Accordingly, this compilation does not show the text of the compiled law as modified. For more information on any modifications, see the series page on the Legislation Register for the compiled law.
Self- repealing provisions
If a provision of the compiled law has been repealed in accordance with a provision of the law, details are included in the endnotes.

AN ACT RELATING TO THE PROVISION OF CERTAIN SERVICES, AND FOR OTHER PURPOSES

PART I - PRELIMINARY

1 Short title
This Act may be cited as the Human Services (Medicare) Act 1973 .

2 Commencement
This Act shall come into operation on the day on which it receives the Royal Assent.

3 Definitions
In this Act, unless the contrary intention appears:

Australia , when used in a geographical sense, includes Norfolk Island, the Territory of Cocos (Keeling) Islands and the Territory of Christmas Island.

authorised officer , in relation to a provision of this Act, means the Chief Executive Medicare or a Departmental employee who is appointed by the Chief Executive Medicare under section 8M to be an authorised officer for the purposes of that provision.

benefit includes:

(a) a pension, allowance, concession or payment; and

(b) a card entitling its holder to a concession or a payment of any kind.

Chief Executive Centrelink has the same meaning as in the Human Services (Centrelink) Act 1997 .

Chief Executive Medicare means the Chief Executive Medicare referred to in section 4.

constable means a member or special member of the Australian Federal Police or a member of the police force or police service of a State or Territory.

data includes:

(a) information in any form; and

(b) any program (or part of a program).

data held in a computer includes:

(a) data held in any removable data storage device for the time being held in a computer; or

(b) data held in a data storage device on a computer network of which the computer forms a part.

data storage device means a thing containing, or designed to contain, data for use by a computer.

dental benefit has the same meaning as in the Dental Benefits Act 2008 .

Departmental employee means an APS employee in the Department.

Note: APS employee is defined in the Acts Interpretation Act 1901 .

evidential material means a thing relevant to a relevant offence or relevant civil contravention, including such a thing in an electronic form.

function includes power.

medicare benefit means a medicare benefit under Part II of the Health Insurance Act 1973 .

medicare functions , in relation to the Chief Executive Medicare, has the meaning given by section 6.

medicare program has the meaning given by section 41G.

occupier , in relation to premises comprising a vessel, vehicle or aircraft, means the person apparently in charge of the vessel, vehicle or aircraft.

officer assisting , in relation to a warrant under Division 4 of Part IID, means:

(a) a person who is a Departmental employee and who is assisting in executing the warrant; or

(b) a person who is not a Departmental employee and who has been authorised by the relevant authorised officer to assist in executing the warrant.

perform includes exercise.

pharmaceutical benefit means a pharmaceutical benefit as defined in Part VII of the National Health Act 1953 .

premises includes a place and a conveyance.

relevant civil contravention has the same meaning as in subsection 124B(1) of the Health Insurance Act 1973 .

relevant offence is defined in section 3A.

Secretary means the Secretary of the Department.

seize includes secure against interference.

service delivery functions , in relation to the Chief Executive Medicare, has the meaning given by section 7.

thing includes a substance.

warrant premises means premises in relation to which a warrant under Division 4 of Part IID is in force.

3A Definitions of relevant offence

(1) For the purposes of this Act other than Divisions 2 and 3 of Part IID, a relevant offence is:

(a) an offence against the Health Insurance Act 1973 ; or

(b) an offence against Part VII of the National Health Act 1953 ; or

(ba) an offence against the Health and Other Services (Compensation) Act 1995 ; or

(bb) an offence against the Medical Indemnity Act 2002 ; or

(bc) an offence against the Dental Benefits Act 2008 ; or

(bd) an offence against the Midwife Professional Indemnity (Commonwealth Contribution) Scheme Act 2010 ; or

(c) an offence against section 6 of the Crimes Act 1914 , or section 11.1, 11.4 or 11.5 of the Criminal Code , that relates to an offence referred to in paragraph (a), (b), (ba), (bb), (bc) or (bd).

(2) For the purposes of Division 2 of Part IID, a relevant offence is:

(a) an offence against Division 3 of Part IIBA or section 128A, 128B, 129 or 129AA of the Health Insurance Act 1973 ; or

(b) an offence against subsection 84L(1) or (2) or section 103 of the National Health Act 1953 ; or

(ba) an offence against the Medical Indemnity Act 2002 ; or

(bb) an offence against section 50, 51, 52, 53 or 54 of the Dental Benefits Act 2008 ; or

(bc) an offence against the Midwife Professional Indemnity (Commonwealth Contribution) Scheme Act 2010 ; or

(c) an offence against section 6 of the Crimes Act 1914 , or section 11.1, 11.4 or 11.5 of the Criminal Code , that relates to an offence referred to in paragraph (a), (b), (ba), (bb) or (bc); or

(d) an offence against section 134.1, 134.2, 135.1, 135.2, 135.4, 136.1, 137.1, 137.2, 145.2 or 145.3 of the Criminal Code that relates to:

(i) a claim for payment in respect of the rendering of a professional service or dental service; or

(ii) an indemnity scheme payment; or

(iii) a Commonwealth contribution (within the meaning of the Midwife Professional Indemnity (Commonwealth Contribution) Scheme Act 2010).

(2A) For the purposes of Division 3 of Part IID, a relevant offence is:

(a) an offence against Division 3 of Part IIBA or section 128A, 128B, 129 or 129AA of the Health Insurance Act 1973 ; or

(b) an offence against subsection 84L(1) or (2) or section 103 of the National Health Act 1953 ; or

(c) an offence against the Health and Other Services (Compensation) Act 1995 ; or

(ca) an offence against the Medical Indemnity Act 2002 ; or

(cb) an offence against section 50, 51, 52, 53 or 54 of the Dental Benefits Act 2008 ; or

(cc) an offence against the Midwife Professional Indemnity (Commonwealth Contribution) Scheme Act 2010 ; or

(d) an offence against section 6 of the Crimes Act 1914 , or section 11.1, 11.4 or 11.5 of the Criminal Code , that relates to an offence referred to in paragraph (a), (b), (c), (ca), (cb) or (cc); or

(e) an offence against section 134.1, 134.2, 135.1, 135.2, 135.4, 136.1, 137.1, 137.2, 145.2 or 145.3 of the Criminal Code that relates to:

(i) a claim for payment in respect of the rendering of a professional service or dental service; or

(ii) an indemnity scheme payment; or

(iii) a Commonwealth contribution (within the meaning of the Midwife Professional Indemnity (Commonwealth Contribution) Scheme Act 2010).

(3) In subsections (2) and (2A):

dental service has the same meaning as in the Dental Benefits Act 2008 .

indemnity scheme payment has the same meaning as in the Medical Indemnity Act 2002 .

professional service has the same meaning as in the Health Insurance Act 1973 .

3B Norfolk Island
This Act extends to Norfolk Island.

PART IIA - CHIEF EXECUTIVE MEDICARE

4 Chief Executive Medicare

(1) There is to be a Chief Executive Medicare.

(2) The Chief Executive Medicare is to be a person who is:

(a) an SES employee in the Department; and

(b) specified in a written instrument made by the Secretary.

(3) A person must not be specified in an instrument under paragraph (2)(b) if the person is, or is acting as:

(a) the Chief Executive Centrelink; or

(b) the Child Support Registrar.

(4) An instrument under paragraph (2)(b) is not a legislative instrument.

4A Acting Chief Executive Medicare

(1) The Secretary may appoint an SES employee in the Department to act as the Chief Executive Medicare:

(a) during a vacancy in the position of Chief Executive Medicare (whether or not an appointment has previously been made to the position); or

(b) during any period, or during all periods, when the Chief Executive Medicare:

(i) is absent from duty or from Australia; or

(ii) is, for any reason, unable to perform the duties of the position.

Note: For rules that apply to acting appointments, see sections 33AB and 33A of the Acts Interpretation Act 1901 .

(2) A person must not be appointed under subsection (1) if the person is, or is acting as:

(a) the Chief Executive Centrelink; or

(b) the Child Support Registrar.

5 Functions of Chief Executive Medicare

Functions-general

(1) The Chief Executive Medicare has the following functions:

(a) the medicare functions mentioned in section 6;

(b) the service delivery functions mentioned in section 7;

(c) any functions conferred on the Chief Executive Medicare under any other Act;

(e) any functions that are prescribed by the regulations;

(f) to do anything incidental to or conducive to the performance of any of the above functions.

Parallel function

(3) A function prescribed by regulations made for the purposes of paragraph (1)(e) may be a specified function that another person (the primary person) has under a law of the Commonwealth.

(4) When the specified function is performed by the Chief Executive Medicare, the function is, for the purposes of that or any other law of the Commonwealth, taken to have been performed by the primary person.

(5) The performance of the specified function by the Chief Executive Medicare does not prevent the performance of the function under the law of the Commonwealth by the primary person.

(6) For the purposes of subsection (3), it is immaterial whether the specified function is a function that can be delegated.

(7) For the purposes of subsection (3), it is immaterial whether the specified function is a function under a law administered by the Minister.

(8) Subsection (3) does not limit paragraph (1)(e).

(9) Subsections (6) and (7) are enacted for the avoidance of doubt.

Function of acting on behalf of another person

(10) A function prescribed by regulations made for the purposes of paragraph (1)(e) may be a function of acting on behalf of another person (the primary person) in the performance of a function that the primary person may perform, whether under a law of the Commonwealth or otherwise.

(11) For the purposes of subsection (10), it is immaterial whether a function that the primary person may perform is a function that can be delegated.

(12) For the purposes of subsection (10), it is immaterial whether a function that the primary person may perform under a law of the Commonwealth is a function under a law administered by the Minister.

(13) For the purposes of subsection (10), it is immaterial whether a function that the primary person may perform otherwise than under a law of the Commonwealth is a function that is within the responsibilities of the Minister.

(14) Subsection (10) does not limit paragraph (1)(e).

(15) Subsections (10) to (14) are enacted for the avoidance of doubt.

6 Chief Executive Medicare's medicare functions

The Chief Executive Medicare's medicare functions are the functions conferred on the Chief Executive Medicare by or under the Health Insurance Act 1973 .

7 Chief Executive Medicare's service delivery functions

The Chief Executive Medicare's service delivery functions are as follows:

(a) to provide services, benefits, programs or facilities that are provided for by the Commonwealth for a purpose for which the Parliament has the power to make laws;

(b) to provide services, benefits, programs or facilities that are provided for by a person or body other than the Commonwealth for a purpose for which the Parliament has the power to make laws.

7A Agreements about performance of Chief Executive Medicare's functions

The Secretary of the Department may enter into a written agreement with the Secretary of another Department about the performance of any of the Chief Executive Medicare's functions.

8AC Delegation

(1) The Chief Executive Medicare may, by writing, delegate to a Departmental employee all or any of the functions of the Chief Executive Medicare under this Act or any other Act.

(1A) For the purposes of subsection (1), it is immaterial whether a function of the Chief Executive Medicare is a function of the kind mentioned in subsection 5(3) or (10).

(2) However, the Chief Executive Medicare must not delegate functions conferred on him or her under another Act if the delegation is inconsistent with the express provisions of that Act.

(3) The Chief Executive Medicare may, by writing, delegate to a Departmental employee all or any of the functions delegated to the Chief Executive Medicare under another Act.

(4) However, the Chief Executive Medicare must not delegate functions delegated to him or her under another Act if the delegation by the Chief Executive Medicare would be inconsistent with the express provisions of that Act.

(5) The Chief Executive Medicare must not delegate functions under subsection (1) or (3) to a Departmental employee who is, or is acting as:

(a) the Chief Executive Centrelink; or

(b) the Child Support Registrar.

8AD Commonwealth consent to conferral of functions etc. on Chief Executive Medicare by State and Territory laws

(1) A law of a State or Territory may confer functions, or impose duties, on the Chief Executive

Medicare.

Note: Section 8AF sets out when such a law imposes a duty on the Chief Executive Medicare.

(2) Subsection (1) does not authorise the conferral of a function, or the imposition of a duty, by a law of a State or Territory to the extent to which:

(a) the conferral or imposition, or the authorisation, would contravene any constitutional doctrines restricting the duties that may be imposed on the Chief Executive Medicare; or

(b) the authorisation would otherwise exceed the legislative power of the Commonwealth.

(3) The Chief Executive Medicare cannot perform a duty or function under a law of a State or Territory without the written approval of the Minister.

8AE How duty is imposed on Chief Executive Medicare by State and Territory laws

Application

(1) This section applies if a law of a State or Territory purports to impose a duty on the Chief Executive Medicare.

Note: Section 8AF sets out when such a law imposes a duty on the Chief Executive Medicare.

State or Territory legislative power sufficient to support duty

(2) The duty is taken not to be imposed by this Act (or any other law of the Commonwealth) to the extent to which:

(a) imposing the duty is within the legislative powers of the State or Territory concerned; and

(b) imposing the duty by the law of the State or Territory is consistent with the constitutional doctrines restricting the duties that may be imposed on the Chief Executive Medicare.

Note: If this subsection applies, the duty will be taken to be imposed by force of the law of the State or Territory (the Commonwealth having consented under section 8AD to the imposition of the duty by that law).

Commonwealth legislative power sufficient to support duty but State or Territory legislative powers are not

(3) If, to ensure the validity of the purported imposition of the duty, it is necessary that the duty be imposed by a law of the Commonwealth (rather than by the law of the State or Territory), the duty is taken to be imposed by this Act to the extent necessary to ensure that validity.

(4) If, because of subsection (3), this Act is taken to impose the duty, it is the intention of the Parliament to rely on all powers available to it under the Constitution to support the imposition of the duty by this Act.

(5) The duty is taken to be imposed by this Act in accordance with subsection (3) only to the extent to which imposing the duty:

(a) is within the legislative powers of the Commonwealth; and

(b) is consistent with the constitutional doctrines restricting the duties that may be imposed on the Chief Executive Medicare.

(6) Subsections (1) to (5) do not limit section 8AD.

8AF When State and Territory laws impose a duty on Chief Executive Medicare

For the purposes of sections 8AD and 8AE, a law of a State or Territory imposes a duty on the Chief Executive Medicare if:

(a) the law confers a function on the Chief Executive Medicare; and

(b) the circumstances in which the function is conferred give rise to an obligation on the Chief Executive Medicare to perform the function.

8B Chief Executive Medicare may be assisted by Departmental employees

A Departmental employee may assist the Chief Executive Medicare in the performance of any of the functions of the Chief Executive Medicare.

PART IID - INVESTIGATIVE POWERS OF CHIEF EXECUTIVE MEDICARE

Division 1 - Preliminary

8K Crown to be bound
(1) This Part binds the Crown in all its capacities.
(2) Nothing in this Part renders the Crown in any of its capacities liable to be prosecuted.

8L Authorisation to exercise powers under this Part
(1) The Chief Executive Medicare may, by instrument in writing, authorise the powers under this Part to be exercised in connection with an investigation that the Chief Executive Medicare is conducting in the performance of his or her functions.
(2) Powers under this Part must not be exercised unless they are exercised in connection with an investigation for which such an authorisation is in force.

8M Authorised officers
The Chief Executive Medicare may, by signed instrument, appoint a Departmental employee to be an authorised officer for the purposes of exercising:
(a) the powers of an authorised officer under this Act; or
(b) such of those powers as are specified in the instrument.

8N Identity cards
(1) The Chief Executive Medicare may cause to be issued to each authorised officer an identity card.
(2) An identity card must:
(a) be in a form approved in writing by the Chief Executive Medicare; and
(b) incorporate a recent photograph of the authorised officer.
(3) A person who ceases to be an authorised officer must, as soon as practicable after so ceasing, return his or her identity card to the Chief Executive Medicare.
(4) A person must not fail to return his or her identity card as required by subsection (3).
Penalty: 1 penalty unit.
Note: Under subsection 4D(1) of the Crimes Act 1914 , this penalty is only a maximum penalty for the offence.
(5) Subsection (4) does not apply if the person has a reasonable excuse.
(6) An offence under subsection (4) is an offence of strict liability.
Note: For strict liability, see section 6.1 of the Criminal Code .

Division 2 - General power to obtain information

8P Chief Executive Medicare may obtain information etc.
(1) An authorised officer may require a person to give information or produce a document that is in the person's custody, or under the person's control, to the Chief Executive Medicare if the authorised officer has reasonable grounds for believing that:

(a) a relevant offence or relevant civil contravention has been or is being committed; and

(b) the information or document is relevant to the offence or contravention.

(2) The requirement must be by notice in writing given to the person.

Note: Sections 28A and 29 of the Acts Interpretation Act 1901 provide how a notice may be given. In particular, the notice may be given to an individual by:

· delivering it personally; or

· leaving it at the person's last known address; or

· sending it by pre- paid post to the person's last known address.

(3) Subject to subsection (4), the power under this section to require information to be given or documents to be produced does not include:

(a) the power to require information to be given about the contents of a part of a record that is a part containing clinical details relating to a patient; or

(b) the power to require production of a part of a record that contains such clinical details.

(4) Subsection (3) does not apply if:

(a) the person being required to give information or produce documents is the patient to whom the clinical details relate; and

(b) the information or documents relate to:

(i) a service the person has received in respect of which medicare benefit or dental benefit has been claimed; or

(ii) a pharmaceutical benefit supplied to, or in respect of, the person.

8Q Content of notices

(1) The notice must specify:

(a) how the person is to give the information or how the document is to be produced; and

(b) the period within which the person is to give the information, or to produce the document, to the Chief Executive Medicare; and

(c) the Departmental employee (if any) to whom the information is to be given or the document is to be produced; and

(d) that the notice is given under section 8P.

(2) The period specified under paragraph (1)(b) must end at least 14 days after the notice is given.

(3) The notice may require the person to give the information by appearing before a specified Departmental employee to answer questions.

(4) If the notice requires the person to appear before a Departmental employee, the notice must specify a time and a place for the person to appear. The time must be at least 14 days after the notice is given.

8R Offences

(1) A person must not refuse or fail to comply with a notice under section 8P.

Penalty: Imprisonment for 6 months.

(1A) However, the person is only required to comply with the notice to the extent that the person is capable of doing so.

Note: The defendant bears an evidential burden in relation to the matter in subsection (1A). See subsection 13.3(3) of the Criminal Code .

(1B) Subsection (1) does not apply if the person has a reasonable excuse.

Note: The defendant bears an evidential burden in relation to the matter in subsection (1B). See subsection 13.3(3) of the Criminal Code .

(2) An offence under subsection (1) is an offence of strict liability.

Note: For strict liability, see section 6.1 of the Criminal Code .

(3) Without limiting what may be taken to be a reasonable excuse for the purposes of subsection (1B), it is, for the purposes of that subsection, a reasonable excuse for refusing or failing to comply with the notice if compliance would have the effect of disclosing the contents of a part of a record that is a part containing clinical details relating to a patient.

8RA Use of information

Scope

(1) This section applies to information that is:

(a) given in accordance with a notice under section 8P; or

(b) contained in a document produced in accordance with a notice under section 8P.

Use of information

(2) The information may be used or disclosed for purposes in connection with:

(a) the exercise of a power under section 124F of the Health Insurance Act 1973 ; or

(b) the exercise of a power under section 124FF of the Health Insurance Act 1973 ; or

(c) the exercise of a power under section 133 of the National Health Act 1953 .

(3) Subsection (2) does not, by implication, limit the purposes for which the information may otherwise be used or disclosed.

8S Self- incrimination

(1) A person is not excused from giving information or producing a document pursuant to a notice under section 8P on the ground that the information, or production of the document, may tend to incriminate the person.

(2) In any criminal proceeding:

(a) evidence of any information given or document produced pursuant to a notice under section 8P; and

(b) evidence of any information, document or thing obtained as a direct or indirect result of the person having given the information or produced the document;

cannot be used against the person. However, this subsection does not apply to a proceeding for an offence against section 8R or an offence against section 137.1 or 137.2 of the Criminal Code that relates to a notice under section 8P of this Act.

8T Exemption

This Division does not require a person to give information or produce a document to the extent that, in doing so, the person would contravene a law of the Commonwealth (other than a law of a Territory).

Division 3 - Searches in relation to possible relevant offences and relevant civil contraventions

8U Authorised officers may conduct searches for the purpose of monitoring compliance

(1) Subject to this Division, if an authorised officer has reasonable grounds for believing that a relevant offence or relevant civil contravention is being committed, or has been committed within the previous 60 days, he or she may:

(a) with the consent of the occupier, enter, at any reasonable time of the day or night, any premises that the authorised officer has reasonable grounds to believe are premises to which this section applies; and

(b) exercise his or her powers under section 8V;

to the extent that it is reasonably necessary for the purpose of ascertaining whether the relevant offence or relevant civil contravention has been or is being committed.

(2) If the occupier does not consent to entry under subsection (1), an authorised officer must not enter the premises without a search warrant.

(3) The authorised officer must not under subsection (1) enter premises that are a residence unless the occupier of the premises has consented to the entry.

(4) In deciding the extent to which it is reasonably necessary to enter premises under subsection (1), an authorised officer must consider whether it is practicable to ascertain whether the relevant offence or relevant civil contravention in question has been or is being committed by:

(a) the authorised officer entering the premises with the occupier's consent; or

(b) the occupier giving information without the authorised officer entering the premises.

(5) This section applies to premises at which activities have been or are being carried out that are associated with:

(a) rendering services in respect of which medicare benefits or dental benefits have been paid or may be payable; or

(b) the prescription for the supply of, or the supply of, pharmaceutical benefits.

(6) In exercising any power under this section an authorised officer must, as soon as practicable, give the occupier of the premises a copy of the relevant instrument made by the Chief Executive Medicare under subsection 8L(1).

8V Powers on entering premises

(1) Subject to subsection (4), having entered the premises, the authorised officer may, for the purpose of ascertaining whether the relevant offence or relevant civil contravention is being committed, or has been committed within the previous 60 days, exercise any one or more of the following powers:

(a) to search the premises;

(b) to take photographs (including video recordings) or make sketches of the premises or any thing on the premises (other than a document);

(c) to inspect, examine and take samples of any thing on or in the premises that is a drug, medicine or substance that may be supplied as, or may be an ingredient of, a pharmaceutical benefit;

(d) to take extracts from any document, book, or record on the premises;

(e) to take on to the premises any equipment or material reasonably necessary for the purposes of exercising a power under paragraph (a), (b), (c) or (d);

(f) in relation to certain documents or records on the premises, to exercise any one or more of the powers under subsections (2) and (3).

(2) The authorised officer has power, under paragraph (1)(f), to operate equipment at the premises to see whether:

(a) the equipment; or

(b) a disk, tape or other storage device that:

(i) is at the premises; and

(ii) can be used with or is associated with the equipment;

contains information that is relevant to determining whether the relevant offence or relevant civil contravention has been or is being committed.

(3) If the authorised officer, after operating equipment at the premises, finds that the equipment, or that a disk, tape or other storage device at the premises, contains information of that kind, he or she has power, under paragraph (1)(f):

(a) to operate the facilities to put the information in documentary form and copy the documents so produced; or

(b) if the information can be transferred to a disk, tape or other storage device that:

(i) is brought to the premises; or

(ii) is at the premises and the use of which for the purpose has been agreed to in writing by the occupier of the premises;

to operate the equipment or other facilities to copy the information to the storage device and remove the storage device from the premises.

(4) The powers under this section do not authorise any act in relation to a part of a record that is a part containing clinical details relating to a patient.

8W Authorised officers to produce evidence of identity

(1) The authorised officer is not entitled to exercise any powers under this Division in relation to particular premises unless the authorised officer produces his or her identity card for inspection by the occupier of the premises.

(2) This section does not apply if the occupier is not present at the premises at any time during which the powers are exercised.

Division 4 - Warrants for searches and seizures

8X Relevant offence and relevant civil contravention related searches and seizures

(1) Subject to this Division, if an authorised officer has reasonable grounds for suspecting that there may be on or in any premises evidential material, the authorised officer and an officer assisting may:

(a) enter the premises; and

(b) search the premises for the evidential material; and

(c) if the authorised officer or officer assisting finds the evidential material on or in the premises-seize it.

(2) The authorised officer or officer assisting must not enter the premises unless:

(a) the occupier of the premises has consented to the entry; or

(b) the entry is made under a warrant issued under section 8Y.

8Y Search warrants

(1) If:

(a) an information on oath is laid before a magistrate alleging that an authorised officer suspects on reasonable grounds that there may be on or in any premises particular evidential material; and

(b) the information sets out those grounds;

the magistrate may issue a search warrant in respect of the premises.

(2) The magistrate must not issue the warrant unless he or she has been:

(a) advised what other warrants (if any) have been sought under this Part in respect of those premises in the preceding 5 years; and

(b) given a copy of the relevant instrument made by the Chief Executive Medicare under subsection 8L(1).

(3) The warrant must authorise an authorised officer named in the warrant with such assistance, and by such force, as is necessary and reasonable:

(a) to enter the premises; and

(b) to search the premises for the evidential material; and

(c) if the authorised officer finds the evidential material on or in the premises-to seize it.

(4) The magistrate is not to issue the warrant unless:

(a) the informant or some other person has given to the magistrate, either orally or by affidavit, such further information (if any) as the magistrate requires concerning the grounds on which the issue of the warrant is being sought; and

(b) the magistrate is satisfied that there are reasonable grounds for issuing the warrant; and

(c) the magistrate is satisfied that execution of the warrant will not cause an unreasonable invasion of any patient's privacy.

(5) There must be stated in the warrant:

(a) the purpose for which the warrant is issued, and the nature of the relevant offence or relevant civil contravention in relation to which the entry and search are authorised; and

(b) whether entry is authorised to be made at any time of the day or night or during specified hours of the day or night; and

(c) a description of the kind of evidential material to be seized; and

(d) a day, not later than 7 days after the day of issue of the warrant, upon which the warrant ceases to have effect; and

(e) whether or not the warrant authorises the exercise of powers in relation to records containing clinical details relating to patients.

8Z Warrants may be issued by telephone or other electronic means

(1) If, because of circumstances of urgency, an authorised officer thinks it necessary to do so, the authorised officer may apply to a magistrate for a warrant under subsection 8Y(1) by telephone, telex, fax or other electronic means under this section.

(2) Before applying, the authorised officer must prepare an information of a kind referred to in subsection 8Y(1) that sets out the grounds on which the issue of the warrant is being sought, but may, if it is necessary to do so, make the application before the information has been sworn.

(3) If an application is made to a magistrate under this section and the magistrate, after considering the information and having received and considered such further information (if any) as the magistrate required, is satisfied that:

(a) a warrant in the terms of the application should be issued urgently; or

(b) the delay that would occur if an application were made in person would frustrate the effective execution of the warrant;

the magistrate may complete and sign the same form of warrant that would be issued under section 8Y.

8ZA Formalities relating to warrants issued by telephone or other electronic means

(1) If the magistrate signs a warrant under section 8Z, the magistrate must:

(a) inform the authorised officer of the terms of the warrant; and

(b) inform the authorised officer of the day on which and the time at which the warrant was signed; and

(c) inform the authorised officer of the day not more than 48 hours after the magistrate completes and signs the warrant on which the warrant ceases to have effect; and

(d) record on the warrant the reasons for issuing the warrant.

(2) The authorised officer must:

(a) complete a form of warrant in the same terms as the warrant completed and signed by the magistrate; and

(b) write on it the magistrate's name and the day on which and the time at which the warrant was signed.

(3) The authorised officer must, not later than the day after the date of expiry or execution of the warrant, whichever is the earlier, send to the magistrate:

(a) the form of warrant completed by the authorised officer; and

(b) the information duly sworn in connection with the warrant.

(4) On receiving the documents referred to in subsection (3), the magistrate must:

(a) attach to them the warrant signed by the magistrate; and

(b) deal with the documents in the way in which the magistrate would have dealt with the information if the application for the warrant had been made under section 8Y.

(5) A form of warrant duly completed by an authorised officer under subsection (2), if it is in accordance with the terms of the warrant signed by the magistrate, is authority for any entry, search, seizure or other exercise of a power that the warrant so signed authorises.

(6) If:

(a) it is material in any proceedings for a court to be satisfied that an entry, search, seizure or other exercise of power was authorised in accordance with this section; and

(b) the warrant signed by a magistrate under this section authorising the entry, search, seizure or other exercise of power is not produced in evidence;

the court is to assume, unless the contrary is proved, that the entry, search, seizure or other exercise of power was not authorised by such a warrant.

Division 5 - Provisions relating to execution of search warrants

8ZB Announcement before entry

(1) The authorised officer or an officer assisting must, before any person enters warrant premises under a warrant:

(a) announce that he or she is authorised by the warrant to enter the premises; and

(b) give any person at the premises an opportunity to allow entry to the premises.

(2) The authorised officer or an officer assisting is not required to comply with subsection (1) if he or she believes on reasonable grounds that immediate entry to the premises is required to ensure:

(a) the safety of a person (including the authorised officer or the officer assisting); or

(b) that the effective execution of the warrant is not frustrated.

8ZC Availability of assistance and use of force in executing a warrant

In executing a warrant:

(a) the authorised officer may obtain such assistance; and

(b) an officer assisting who is a constable may use such force against persons and things; and

(c) the authorised officer and an officer assisting who is not a constable may use such force against things;

as is necessary and reasonable in the circumstances.

8ZD Details of warrant to be given to occupier etc.

(1) If a warrant is being executed and the occupier of the warrant premises, or another person who apparently represents the occupier, is present at the premises, the authorised officer or an officer assisting must make available to that person a copy of the warrant.

(2) The authorised officer must identify himself or herself to the person at the premises.

(3) The copy of the warrant referred to in subsection (1) need not include the signature of the magistrate who issued it or the seal of the relevant court.

8ZE Specific powers available to officers executing warrants

(1) In executing a warrant, the authorised officer or an officer assisting may:

(a) for a purpose incidental to execution of the warrant; or

(b) if the occupier of the warrant premises consents in writing;

take photographs (including video recordings) of the premises or of things at the premises.

(2) If a warrant is being executed, the authorised officer and the officers assisting may, if the warrant is still in force, complete the execution of the warrant after all of them temporarily cease its execution and leave the warrant premises:

(a) for not more than one hour; or

(b) for a longer period if the occupier of the premises consents in writing.

(3) If:

(a) the execution of a warrant is stopped by an order of a court; and

(b) the order is later revoked or reversed on appeal; and

(c) the warrant is still in force;

the execution of the warrant may be completed.

8ZF Use of equipment to examine or process things

(1) The authorised officer or an officer assisting may bring to the warrant premises any equipment reasonably necessary for the examination or processing of a thing found at the premises in order to determine whether it is a thing that may be seized under the warrant.

(2) A thing found at the premises may be moved to another place for examination or processing in order to determine whether it may be seized under a warrant if:

(a) both of the following apply:

(i) it is significantly more practicable to do so having regard to the timeliness and cost of examining or processing the thing at another place and the availability of expert assistance;

(ii) the authorised officer or officer assisting suspects on reasonable grounds that the thing contains or constitutes evidential material; or

(b) the occupier of the premises consents in writing.

(3) If a thing is moved to another place for the purpose of examination or processing under subsection (2), the authorised officer must, if it is practicable to do so:

(a) inform the occupier of the address of the place and the time at which the examination or processing will be carried out; and

(b) allow the occupier or his or her representative to be present during the examination or processing.

(4) The authorised officer need not comply with paragraph (3)(a) or (b) if he or she believes on reasonable grounds that to do so might:

(a) endanger the safety of a person; or

(b) prejudice an investigation or prosecution.

(5) The thing may be moved to another place for examination or processing for no longer than 14 days.

(6) An authorised officer may apply to a magistrate for one or more extensions of that time if the authorised officer believes on reasonable grounds that the thing cannot be examined or processed within 14 days or that time as previously extended.

(7) The authorised officer must give notice of the application to the occupier of the premises, and the occupier is entitled to be heard in relation to the application.

(8) A single extension cannot exceed 7 days.

(9) The authorised officer or an officer assisting may operate equipment already at the warrant premises to carry out the examination or processing of a thing found at the premises in order to determine whether it is a thing that may be seized under the warrant if the authorised officer or officer assisting believes on reasonable grounds that:

(a) the equipment is suitable for the examination or processing; and

(b) the examination or processing can be carried out without damage to the equipment or the thing.

8ZG Use of electronic equipment at premises

(1) The authorised officer or an officer assisting may operate electronic equipment at the warrant premises to access data (including data not held at the premises) if he or she suspects on reasonable grounds that the data constitutes evidential material.

Note: An authorised officer can obtain an order requiring a person with knowledge of a computer or computer system to provide assistance: see section 8ZGB.

(2) If the authorised officer or officer assisting suspects on reasonable grounds that any data accessed by operating the electronic equipment constitutes evidential material, he or she may:

(a) copy any or all of the data accessed by operating the electronic equipment to a disk, tape or other associated device brought to the premises; or

(b) if the occupier of the premises agrees in writing-copy any or all of the data accessed by operating the electronic equipment to a disk, tape or other associated device at the premises; and take the device from the premises.

(3) If:

(a) the authorised officer or officer assisting takes the device from the premises; and

(b) the Chief Executive Medicare is satisfied that:

(i) the reason for the copying of the data no longer exists; or

(ii) a decision has been made not to use the data in evidence;

the Chief Executive Medicare must arrange for:

(c) the removal of the data from any device in the control of a Departmental employee; and

(d) the destruction of any other reproduction of the data in the control of a Departmental employee.

(4) If the authorised officer or an officer assisting, after operating the equipment, finds that evidential material is accessible by doing so, he or she may:

(a) seize the equipment and any disk, tape or other associated device; or

(b) if the material can, by using facilities at the premises, be put in documentary form-operate the facilities to put the material in that form and seize the documents so produced.

(5) An authorised officer or an officer assisting may seize equipment under paragraph (4)(a) only if:

(a) it is not practicable to copy the data as mentioned in subsection (2) or to put the material in documentary form as mentioned in paragraph (4)(b); or

(b) possession by the occupier of the equipment could constitute an offence.

(6) If the authorised officer or an officer assisting suspects on reasonable grounds that:

(a) evidential material may be accessible by operating electronic equipment at the premises; and

(b) expert assistance is required to operate the equipment; and

(c) if he or she does not take action under this subsection, the material may be destroyed, altered or otherwise interfered with;

he or she may do whatever is necessary to secure the equipment, whether by locking it up, placing a guard or otherwise.

(7) The authorised officer or an officer assisting must give notice to the occupier of the premises of his or her intention to secure equipment and of the fact that the equipment may be secured for up to 24 hours.

(8) The equipment may be secured:

(a) for a period not exceeding 24 hours; or

(b) until the equipment has been operated by the expert;

whichever happens first.

(9) If the authorised officer or an officer assisting believes on reasonable grounds that the expert assistance will not be available within 24 hours, he or she may apply to a magistrate for an extension of that period.

(10) The authorised officer or an officer assisting must give notice to the occupier of the premises of his or her intention to apply for an extension, and the occupier is entitled to be heard in relation to the application.

(11) The provisions of Division 4 relating to the issue of warrants apply, with such modifications as are necessary, to the issuing of an extension.

8ZGA Use of electronic equipment at other place

(1) If electronic equipment found at the warrant premises is moved to another place under subsection 8ZF(2), the authorised officer or an officer assisting may operate the equipment to access data (including data held at another place).

(2) If the authorised officer or officer assisting suspects on reasonable grounds that any data accessed by operating the electronic equipment constitutes evidential material, he or she may copy any or all of the data accessed by operating the electronic equipment to a disk, tape or other associated device.

(3) If the Chief Executive Medicare is satisfied that:

(a) the reason for the copying of the data no longer exists; or

(b) a decision has been made not to use the data in evidence;

the Chief Executive Medicare must arrange for:

(c) the removal of the data from any device in the control of a Departmental employee; and

(d) the destruction of any other reproduction of the data in the control of a Departmental employee.

(4) If the authorised officer or an officer assisting, after operating the equipment, finds that evidential material is accessible by doing so, he or she may:

(a) seize the equipment and any disk, tape or other associated device; or

(b) if the material can be put in documentary form-put the material in that form and seize the documents so produced.

(5) An authorised officer or officer assisting may seize equipment under paragraph (4)(a) only if:

(a) it is not practicable to copy the data as mentioned in subsection (2) or to put the material in documentary form as mentioned in paragraph (4)(b); or

(b) possession by the occupier of the equipment could constitute an offence.

8ZGB Person with knowledge of a computer or a computer system to assist access etc.

(1) An authorised officer may apply to a magistrate for an order requiring a specified person to provide any information or assistance that is reasonable and necessary to allow an authorised officer or officer assisting to do one or more of the following:

(a) access data held in, or accessible from, a computer or data storage device that:

(i) is on warrant premises; or

(ii) has been removed from warrant premises under subsection 8ZF(2) and is at another place for examination or processing; or

(iii) has been seized under this Division and is no longer on the warrant premises;

(b) copy data held in, or accessible from, a computer, or data storage device, described in paragraph (a) to another data storage device;

(c) convert into documentary form or another form intelligible to an authorised officer or officer assisting:

(i) data held in, or accessible from, a computer, or data storage device, described in paragraph (a); or

(ii) data held in a data storage device to which the data was copied as described in paragraph (b); or

(iii) data held in a data storage device removed from warrant premises under subsection 8ZG(2).

(2) The magistrate may grant the order if the magistrate is satisfied that:

(a) there are reasonable grounds for suspecting that evidential material is held in, or is accessible from, the computer or data storage device; and

(b) the specified person is:

(i) reasonably suspected of having committed the relevant offence or relevant civil contravention stated in the relevant warrant; or

(ii) the owner or lessee of the computer or device; or

(iii) an employee of the owner or lessee of the computer or device; or

(iv) a person engaged under a contract for services by the owner or lessee of the computer or device; or

(v) a person who uses or has used the computer or device; or

(vi) a person who is or was a system administrator for the system including the computer or device; and

(c) the specified person has relevant knowledge of:

(i) the computer or device or a computer network of which the computer or device forms or formed a part; or

(ii) measures applied to protect data held in, or accessible from, the computer or device.

(3) If:

(a) the computer or data storage device that is the subject of the order is seized under this Division;

and

(b) the order was granted on the basis of an application made before the seizure;

the order does not have effect on or after the seizure.

Note: An application for another order under this section relating to the computer or data storage device may be made after the seizure. If the other order is made after the computer or device has been removed from the warrant premises, that other order can specify conditions relating to the provision of information or assistance.

(4) If the computer or data storage device is not on warrant premises, the order must:

(a) specify the period within which the person must provide the information or assistance; and

(b) specify the place at which the person must provide the information or assistance; and

(c) specify the conditions (if any) determined by the magistrate as the conditions to which the requirement on the person to provide the information or assistance is subject.

(5) A person commits an offence if the person fails to comply with the order.

Penalty for contravention of this subsection: Imprisonment for 2 years.

8ZGC Accessing data held on other premises-notification to occupier of that premises

(1) If:

(a) data that is held on premises other than the warrant premises is accessed under subsection 8ZG(1) or 8ZGA(1); and

(b) it is practicable to notify the occupier of the other premises that the data has been accessed under a warrant;

the authorised officer must:

(c) do so as soon as practicable; and

(d) if the authorised officer has arranged, or intends to arrange, for continued access to the data under subsection 8ZG(2) or (4) or 8ZGA(2) or (4)-include that information in the notification.

(2) A notification under subsection (1) must include sufficient information to allow the occupier of the other premises to contact the authorised officer.

8ZH Compensation for damage to electronic equipment

(1) If:

(a) damage is caused to equipment as a result of it being operated as mentioned in section 8ZF, 8ZG or 8ZGA; and

(b) the damage was caused as a result of:

(i) insufficient care being exercised in selecting the person who was to operate the equipment; or

(ii) insufficient care being exercised by the person operating the equipment;

compensation for the damage is payable to the owner of the equipment.

(2) Compensation is payable out of money appropriated by the Parliament for the purpose.

(3) In determining the amount of compensation payable, regard is to be had to whether the occupier of the warrant premises and his or her employees and agents, if they were available at the time, had provided any warning or guidance as to the operation of the equipment that was appropriate in the circumstances.

8ZI Seizure of things not covered by warrants

If:

(a) in the course of searching, in accordance with a warrant, for particular evidential material, an authorised officer or an officer assisting finds evidential material that the authorised officer or officer assisting believes on reasonable grounds to be:

(i) evidential material in relation to the relevant offence or relevant civil contravention to which the warrant relates, although not the evidential material specified in the warrant; or

(ii) evidential material in relation to another relevant offence or relevant civil contravention; and

(b) the authorised officer or officer assisting believes, on reasonable grounds, that it is necessary to seize that evidential material in order to prevent its concealment, loss or destruction, or its use in committing, continuing or repeating the relevant offence or relevant civil contravention or the other relevant offence or relevant civil contravention;

the warrant is taken to authorise the authorised officer or officer assisting to seize that evidential material.

8ZJ Occupier entitled to observe search

(1) If a warrant in relation to premises is being executed and the occupier of the premises or another person who apparently represents the occupier is present at the premises, the person is entitled to observe the search being conducted.

(2) The right to observe the search being conducted ceases if the person impedes the search.

(3) This section does not prevent 2 or more areas of the premises being searched at the same time.

8ZK Receipts for things seized under warrant

(1) If a thing is seized under a warrant or moved under subsection 8ZF(2), the authorised officer or an officer assisting must provide a receipt for the thing.

(2) If 2 or more things are seized or moved, they may be covered in the one receipt.

8ZL Copies of seized things to be provided

(1) Subject to subsection (2), if an authorised officer or an officer assisting seizes, under Division 4 or this Division:

(a) a document, film, computer file or other thing that can be readily copied; or

(b) a storage device the information in which can be readily copied;

the authorised officer or officer assisting must, if requested to do so by the occupier of the warrant premises or another person who apparently represents the occupier and who is present when the warrant is executed, give a copy of the thing or the information to that person as soon as practicable after the seizure.

(2) Subsection (1) does not apply if the thing that has been seized was seized under paragraph 8ZG(4)(b) or 8ZGA(4)(b).

8ZM Retention of things seized

(1) Subject to any contrary order of a court, if an authorised officer or an officer assisting seizes evidential material under Division 4 or this Division, the authorised officer, officer assisting or the Chief Executive Medicare must return it if:

(a) the reason for its seizure no longer exists; or

(b) a decision is made not to use it in evidence.

(1A) Subsection (1) does not apply if the evidential material is forfeited or forfeitable to the Commonwealth or is the subject of a dispute as to ownership.

(2) The Chief Executive Medicare may, by written instrument, authorise evidential material seized under this Division to be released to the owner, or to the person from whom it was seized, either unconditionally or on such conditions as the Chief Executive Medicare thinks fit.

Division 6 - Miscellaneous

8ZN Patients to be advised of search, seizure etc. of clinical records

(1) If, in the exercise of a power under this Part:

(a) an authorised officer; or

(b) an officer assisting;

examines a record containing clinical details relating to an individual patient, the Chief Executive

Medicare must advise the patient in writing of the examination of the record.

(2) Subsection (1) does not apply if:

(a) so advising the patient would prejudice the investigation in connection with which the powers were exercised; or

(b) the Chief Executive Medicare is unable, after making reasonable inquiries, to locate the patient; or

(c) the examination of the record did not result in:

(i) the authorised officer; or

(ii) the officer assisting;

obtaining any knowledge of any of the clinical details relating to the patient.

8ZO Offence for making false statements in warrants

A person must not make, in an application for a warrant, a statement that the person knows to be false or misleading in a material particular.

Penalty: Imprisonment for 2 years.

Note: Under subsection 4D(1) of the Crimes Act 1914 , this penalty is only a maximum penalty for the offence. Subsection 4B(2) of that Act allows a court to impose an appropriate fine instead of, or in addition to, a term of imprisonment.

8ZP Offences relating to telephone warrants

A person must not:

(a) state in a document that purports to be a form of warrant under section 8Z the name of a magistrate unless that magistrate issued the warrant; or

(b) state on a form of warrant under that section a matter that, to the person's knowledge, departs in a material particular from the form authorised by the magistrate; or

(c) purport to execute, or present to a person, a document that purports to be a form of warrant under that section that the person knows:

(i) has not been approved by a magistrate under that section; or

(ii) to depart in a material particular from the terms authorised by a magistrate under that section; or

(d) send to a magistrate a form of warrant under that section that is not the form of warrant that the person purported to execute.

Penalty: Imprisonment for 2 years.

Note: Under subsection 4D(1) of the Crimes Act 1914 , this penalty is only a maximum penalty for the offence. Subsection 4B(2) of that Act allows a court to impose an appropriate fine instead of, or in addition to, a term of imprisonment.

8ZQ Actions under this Part taken to be in performance of certain functions

(1) For the purposes of this Act, anything done under this Part for a purpose related to the Health Insurance Act 1973 , including investigation of whether benefits are payable under that Act and investigation of compliance with that Act, is taken to have been done in the performance of the Chief Executive Medicare's medicare functions.

(2) For the purposes of this Act and the regulations, anything done under this Part for a purpose related to Part VII of the National Health Act 1953 , including investigation of whether benefits are payable under that Part and investigation of compliance with that Part, is taken to have been done in the performance of the Chief Executive Medicare's functions relating to the provision of pharmaceutical benefits.

8ZR Powers of magistrates

Powers conferred personally

(1) A power conferred on a magistrate by this Part is conferred on the magistrate:

(a) in a personal capacity; and

(b) not as a court or a member of a court.

Powers need not be accepted

(2) The magistrate need not accept the power conferred.

Protection and immunity

(3) A magistrate exercising a power conferred by this Part has the same protection and immunity as if he or she were exercising the power:

(a) as the court of which the magistrate is a member; or

(b) as a member of the court of which the magistrate is a member.

PART VI - MISCELLANEOUS

41C Protection of names and symbols

(1) A person who:

(a) uses the name "medicare" or "Medicare Australia", or a prescribed symbol, in connection with a business, trade, profession or occupation;

(b) sells, offers for sale, exposes for sale or lets for hire, or otherwise has in his or her possession for sale or hire, goods to which the name "medicare" or "Medicare Australia" or a prescribed symbol has been applied;

(c) uses the name "medicare" or "Medicare Australia" or a prescribed symbol in relation to goods or to the promotion, by any means, of the supply or use of goods; or

(d) imports into Australia for sale, or for use for the purposes of any business, trade, profession or occupation, any article to which the name "medicare" or "Medicare Australia" or a prescribed symbol has been applied outside Australia;

commits an offence against this section.

Note: See section 41CA for exceptions.

(2) Where the name "medicare" or "Medicare Australia" or a prescribed symbol:

(a) is used as, or as part of, the name or emblem of an association;

(b) is used as, or as part of, the name or emblem of a newspaper or magazine owned by, or published by or on behalf of, an association; or

(c) is used by an association in connection with any activity of the association with the result of implying that the association is in any way connected with the Commonwealth, the Chief Executive Medicare or the Department;

then:

(d) if the association is a body corporate-the association; or

(e) if the association is not a body corporate-every member of the committee of management or other governing body of the association;

commits an offence against this section.

Note: See section 41CA for exceptions.

(3) A person who commits an offence against this section is punishable, upon conviction:

(a) in the case of a person not being a body corporate-by a fine not exceeding 20 penalty units; or

(b) in the case of a person being a body corporate-by a fine not exceeding 40 penalty units.

(4) The conviction of a person of an offence against this section in respect of the use of a name or prescribed symbol does not prevent a further conviction of that person in respect of the use of that name or prescribed symbol at any time after the first- mentioned conviction.

(5) For the purposes of this section:

(a) a reference to the name "medicare" or "Medicare Australia" is to be read as including a reference to a name or expression that so nearly resembles the name as to be capable of being mistaken for the name; and

(b) a reference to an official "medicare" or "Medicare Australia" symbol is to be read as a reference to a symbol declared by the regulations to be an official "medicare" or "Medicare

Australia" symbol; and

(c) a reference to a prescribed symbol is to be read as a reference to an emblem, brand, design, symbol, logo or mark that:

(i) is identical with an official "medicare" or "Medicare Australia" symbol; or

(ii) so nearly resembles an official "medicare" or "Medicare Australia" symbol as to be capable of being mistaken for an official "medicare" or "Medicare Australia" symbol; and

(d) a name or a prescribed symbol shall be deemed to be applied to goods if it:

(i) is woven in, impressed on, worked into or affixed to the goods; or

(ii) is applied to a covering, label, reel or thing in or with which the goods are supplied; and

(e) a name or a prescribed symbol shall be deemed to be used in relation to goods, or to the promotion of the supply or use of goods, if it is used in a sign, advertisement (whether printed, broadcast or televised), invoice, catalogue, price list or other document in relation to goods; and

(f) the reference in paragraph (d) to a covering includes a reference to a stopper, glass, bottle, vessel, box, capsule, case, frame or wrapper and the reference in that paragraph to a label includes a reference to a band or ticket.

(7) Subject to subsection (9), nothing in this section affects any rights conferred by law on a person in respect of:

(a) a trade mark registered under the Trade Marks Act 1955 , being a trade mark that was so registered before the date of commencement of this section; or

(b) a design registered under the Designs Act 2003 , being a design that was registered under the Designs Act 1906 before the commencement of this section.

(8) Subject to subsection (9), nothing in this section affects the use, or any rights conferred by law relating to the use, of a name or a symbol on or after the date of commencement of this section if:

(a) within the prescribed period before that date, the person used the name or symbol in good faith in a manner mentioned in subsection (1) or (2); or

(b) immediately before that date the person would have been entitled to prevent another person from passing off, by means of the use of that name or symbol or of a similar name or symbol, goods or services as the goods or services of that first- mentioned person.

(9) No action or proceeding, whether criminal or civil, lies against the Commonwealth for or in relation to the use by the Commonwealth of the name "medicare" or "Medicare Australia" or of an official "medicare" or "Medicare Australia" symbol.

(10) To the extent that subsection (9) results in an acquisition of property from any person, the Commonwealth is liable to pay to that person such compensation as is agreed upon between them or, in default of agreement, as is determined by the Federal Court of Australia.

(11) The Federal Court of Australia has jurisdiction with respect of matters arising under subsection (10).

41CA Authorisations for purposes of section 41C

(1) Subsection 41C(1) or (2) does not apply to conduct engaged in by a person in accordance with an authorisation (including any conditions) in force under subsection (2) of this section in relation to the person.

Note: A defendant bears an evidential burden in relation to the matter in subsection (1): see subsection 13.3(3) of the Criminal Code .

(2) For the purposes of subsection (1), the Secretary may, by writing, authorise specified persons to engage in specified conduct. The authorisation may make the conduct subject to specified conditions.

Note: For specification by class, see subsection 33(3AB) of the Acts Interpretation Act 1901 .

(3) An authorisation under subsection (2) ceases to be in force in relation to a person if the person contravenes a condition of the authorisation that applies to the person.

(4) Subsection (3) does not limit the application of subsection 33(3) of the Acts Interpretation Act 1901 in relation to an authorisation under subsection (2) of this section.

Note: Subsection 33(3) of the Acts Interpretation Act 1901 deals with revocation and variation etc.

of instruments.

Delegation

(5) The Secretary may, by writing, delegate the Secretary's powers under subsection (2) to:

(a) the Chief Executive Medicare; or

(b) any other APS employee in the Department; or

(c) an APS employee in the Department administered by the Minister administering the Health Insurance Act 1973 .

Note: The expression APS employee is defined in section 2B of the Acts Interpretation Act 1901 .

(6) A delegate must comply with any written directions of the Secretary.

Authorisation not a legislative instrument

(7) An authorisation under subsection (2) is not a legislative instrument.

41D Forfeiture of articles etc.

All articles or goods by means of which, or in relation to which, an offence against subsection 41C(1) is committed are forfeited to the Commonwealth.

41E Sections 41C and 41D not to limit other laws

The provisions of sections 41C and 41D are in addition to, and not in substitution for, the provisions of any other law (whether a law of the Commonwealth or a law of a State or Territory) that confers rights or powers on the Commonwealth, including, but without limiting the generality of the foregoing, rights or powers to institute civil or criminal proceedings for the protection of the property or interests of the Commonwealth.

41F Chief Executive Medicare may charge for services

The Chief Executive Medicare may charge fees for services he or she provides in connection with the performance of his or her functions.

41G Medicare programs

For the purposes of a law of the Commonwealth, the following are medicare programs :

(a) services, benefits, programs or facilities that are provided for under:

(i) the Health Insurance Act 1973 ; or

(ii) the National Health Act 1953 ; or

(iii) the Dental Benefits Act 2008 ; or

(iv) the Aged Care Act 1997 ; or

(iva) the Aged Care (Transitional Provisions) Act 1997 ; or

(v) the Healthcare Identifiers Act 2010 ; or

(vi) the Private Health Insurance Act 2007 ; or

(vii) the Health and Other Services (Compensation) Act 1995 ;

(b) services, benefits, programs or facilities specified in a legislative instrument made by the Minister for the purposes of this paragraph.

42 Annual report

(1) The annual report on the Department's activities given by the Secretary under section 63 of the Public Service Act 1999 must include:

(a) the number of signed instruments made under section 8M; and

(b) the number of notices in writing given under section 8P; and

(c) the number of notices in writing given to individual patients under section 8P; and

(d) the number of premises entered under section 8U; and

(e) the number of occasions when powers were used under section 8V; and

(f) the number of search warrants issued under section 8Y; and

(g) the number of search warrants issued by telephone or other electronic means under section 8Z; and

(h) the number of patients advised in writing under section 8ZN.

(2) The annual report mentioned in subsection (1) must also include information about the operation of the following Acts during the financial year to which the report relates:

(a) the Medical Indemnity Act 2002 ;

(aa) the Medical Indemnity (Competitive Advantage Payment) Act 2005 ;

(b) the Medical Indemnity (Run- off Cover Support Payment) Act 2004 ;

(c) the Medical Indemnity (UMP Support Payment) Act 2002 ;

(d) the Midwife Professional Indemnity (Commonwealth Contribution) Scheme Act 2010 ;

(e) the Midwife Professional Indemnity (Run- off Cover Support Payment) Act 2010 .

43 Arrangements with States and Territories-magistrates

States

(1) The Governor- General may make arrangements with the Governor of a State in relation to the performance of the functions of a magistrate under this Act by a magistrate of that State.

(2) The Governor- General may arrange with the Governor of a State with whom an arrangement is in force under subsection (1) for the variation or revocation of the arrangement.

Australian Capital Territory

(3) The Governor- General may make arrangements with the Chief Minister of the Australian Capital Territory in relation to the performance of the functions of a magistrate under this Act by a magistrate of the Australian Capital Territory.

(4) The Governor- General may arrange with the Chief Minister of the Australian Capital Territory for the variation or revocation of an arrangement in force under subsection (3).

Northern Territory

(5) The Governor- General may make arrangements with the Administrator of the Northern Territory in relation to the performance of the functions of a magistrate under this Act by a magistrate of the Northern Territory.

(6) The Governor- General may arrange with the Administrator of the Northern Territory for the variation or revocation of an arrangement in force under subsection (5).

Gazettal

(7) A copy of each instrument by which an arrangement under this section is made, varied or revoked is to be published in the Gazette .

Legislative instruments

(8) An instrument by which an arrangement under this section is made, varied or revoked is not a legislative instrument.

43A Multiple secrecy provisions

Scope

(1) This section applies to particular information if:

(a) the information is subject to a regulatory regime under a designated program Act (the first program Act); and

(b) the information is also subject to a regulatory regime under another designated program Act (the second program Act).

For the purposes of this subsection, in determining whether particular information is subject to a regulatory regime under a designated program Act, disregard whether the information is subject to a regulatory regime under any other designated program Act.

Disclosure or use of information etc.

(2) If:

(a) the Secretary, the Chief Executive Medicare or a Departmental employee:

(i) discloses the information; or

(ii) uses the information; or

(iii) makes a record of the information; and

(b) the Secretary, the Chief Executive Medicare or the Departmental employee, as the case may be, does so without contravening the first program Act;

the disclosure, use, or making of the record, as the case may be, does not contravene the second program Act.

Definitions

(3) In this section:

designated program Act means:

(a) the A New Tax System (Family Assistance) (Administration) Act 1999 ; or

(b) the Aged Care Act 1997 ; or

(ba) the Australian Immunisation Register Act 2015 ; or

(c) the Child Support (Assessment) Act 1989 ; or

(d) the Child Support (Registration and Collection) Act 1988 ; or

(e) the Dental Benefits Act 2008 ; or

(f) the Disability Services Act 1986 ; or

(g) the Health Insurance Act 1973 ; or

(h) the Medical Indemnity Act 2002 ; or

(i) the Midwife Professional Indemnity (Commonwealth Contribution) Scheme Act 2010 ; or

(j) the National Health Act 1953 ; or

(k) the Paid Parental Leave Act 2010 ; or

(l) the Private Health Insurance Act 2007 ; or

(m) the Social Security (Administration) Act 1999 ; or

(n) the Student Assistance Act 1973 ; or

(o) an Act specified in a legislative instrument made by the Minister for the purposes of this paragraph.

disclose means disclose, divulge or communicate.

44 Regulations

The Governor- General may make regulations, not inconsistent with this Act, prescribing all matters required or permitted by this Act to be prescribed or necessary or convenient to be prescribed for carrying out or giving effect to this Act.

ENDNOTES

Endnote 1-About the endnotes

The endnotes provide information about this compilation and the compiled law.

The following endnotes are included in every compilation:

Endnote 1-About the endnotes

Endnote 2-Abbreviation key

Endnote 3-Legislation history

Endnote 4-Amendment history

Abbreviation key-Endnote 2

The abbreviation key sets out abbreviations that may be used in the endnotes.

Legislation history and amendment history-Endnotes 3 and 4

Amending laws are annotated in the legislation history and amendment history.

The legislation history in endnote 3 provides information about each law that has amended (or will amend) the compiled law. The information includes commencement details for amending laws and details of any application, saving or transitional provisions that are not included in this compilation.

The amendment history in endnote 4 provides information about amendments at the provision (generally section or equivalent) level. It also includes information about any provision of the compiled law that has been repealed in accordance with a provision of the law.

Editorial changes

The Legislation Act 2003 authorises First Parliamentary Counsel to make editorial and presentational changes to a compiled law in preparing a compilation of the law for registration. The changes must not change the effect of the law. Editorial changes take effect from the compilation registration date.

If the compilation includes editorial changes, the endnotes include a brief outline of the changes in general terms. Full details of any changes can be obtained from the Office of Parliamentary Counsel.

Misdescribed amendments

A misdescribed amendment is an amendment that does not accurately describe the amendment to be made. If, despite the misdescription, the amendment can be given effect as intended, the amendment is incorporated into the compiled law and the abbreviation "(md)" added to the details of the amendment included in the amendment history.

If a misdescribed amendment cannot be given effect as intended, the abbreviation "(md not incorp)" is added to the details of the amendment included in the amendment history.

Endnote 2-Abbreviation key

ad = added or inserted	o = order(s)
am = amended	Ord = Ordinance
amdt = amendment	orig = original
c = clause(s)	par = paragraph(s)/subparagraph(s)
C[x] = Compilation No. x	/sub- subparagraph(s)
Ch = Chapter(s)	pres = present
def = definition(s)	prev = previous
Dict = Dictionary	(prev…) = previously
disallowed = disallowed by Parliament	Pt = Part(s)
Div = Division(s)	r = regulation(s)/rule(s)
ed = editorial change	reloc = relocated
exp = expires/expired or ceases/ceased to have	renum = renumbered
effect	rep = repealed
F = Federal Register of Legislation	rs = repealed and substituted
gaz = gazette	s = section(s)/subsection(s)
LA = Legislation Act 2003	Sch = Schedule(s)
LIA = Legislative Instruments Act 2003	Sdiv = Subdivision(s)
(md) = misdescribed amendment can be given	SLI = Select Legislative Instrument
effect	SR = Statutory Rules
(md not incorp) = misdescribed amendment	Sub- Ch = Sub- Chapter(s)
cannot be given effect	SubPt = Subpart(s)
mod = modified/modification	underlining = whole or part not
No. = Number(s)	commenced or to be commenced

Endnote 3-Legislation history

Act	Number and year	Assent	Commencement	Application, saving and transitional provisions
Health Insurance Commission Act 1973	41, 1974	8 Aug 1974	8 Aug 1974	
Health Insurance Commission Amendment Act 1976	61, 1976	5 June 1976	5 June 1976	—
Administrative Changes (Consequential Provisions) Act 1976	91, 1976	20 Sept 1976	s. 3: (a)	s. 4

| Health Insurance Commission Amendment Act (No. 2) 1976 | 100, 1976 | 29 Sept 1976 | s. 6: Royal Assent s. 9: 1 Apr 1977 Remainder: 1 July 1976 | — |

| Administrative Changes (Consequential Provisions) Act 1978 | 36, 1978 | 12 June 1978 | 12 June 1978 | s. 8 |

| Health Insurance Commission Amendment Act 1978 | 134, 1978 | 31 Oct 1978 | 1 Nov 1978 | ss. 30–36 |

| Health Insurance Amendment Act 1979 | 53, 1979 | 14 June 1979 | ss. 5–7: 1 Sept 1979 s. 9 and Part III (ss. 11, 12): 1 July 1979 Remainder: Royal Assent | — |

| Health Legislation Amendment Act 1983 | 54, 1983 | 1 Oct 1983 | ss. 1–3, 4(1), 31(1), 32(4)–(8), 39, 45, 64–67, 70–82, 83(1), 85–88, 89(2), 95–99, 115(1), 119(1), 120(1), 123, 124, 126, 128 and 129: Royal Assent Remainder: 1 Feb 1984 | ss. 67(2), 74(2), 83(3), 84(2), 87, 135 and 136 |

| Conciliation and Arbitration Amendment Act (No. 2) 1983 | 115, 1983 | 16 Dec 1983 | s. 41: 1 June 1984 (see Gazette 1984, No. S201) (b) | — |

| Public Service Reform Act 1984 | 63, 1984 | 25 June 1984 | s. 151(1): 1 July 1984 (see Gazette 1984, No. S245) (c) | s. 151(9) |

| Statute Law (Miscellaneous Provisions) Act (No. 1) 1985 | 65, 1985 | 5 June 1985 | s. 3: 3 July 1985 (d) | — |

| Health Legislation Amendment Act (No. 2) 1985 | 167, 1985 | 16 Dec 1985 | ss. 1–25, 26(2), 27, 37, 38, 42, 43, 55, 57, 65–70 and 72–74: Royal Assent s. 28: 1 Feb 1984 s. 30: 5 Sept 1985 ss. 58–64: 1 May 1985 Remainder: 22 Feb 1986 (see Gazette 1986, No. S64) | ss. 65 and 66 |

| Health Legislation Amendment Act 1986 | 75, 1986 | 24 June 1986 | Part III (ss. 55, 56): 22 July 1986 (e) | — |

| Commonwealth Employees' Rehabilitation and Compensation Act 1988 | 75, 1988 | 24 June 1988 | ss. 1 and 2: Royal Assent ss. 4(1), 68–97, 99 and 100: 1 July 1988 (see Gazette 1988, No. S196) Remainder: 1 Dec 1988 (see Gazette 1988, No. S196) | — |

| Statutory Instruments (Tabling and Disallowance) Legislation Amendment Act 1988 | 99, 1988 | 2 Dec 1988 | 2 Dec 1988 | — |

| Health Legislation (Pharmaceutical Benefits) Amendment Act 1991 | 119, 1991 | 27 June 1991 | s. 3: Royal Assent (f) ss. 4 (in part) and 5: 1 July 1991 (f) s. 4 (in part): 1 Aug 1991 (see Gazette 1991, No. S209) (f) | — |

| Industrial Relations Legislation Amendment Act 1991 | 122, 1991 | 27 June 1991 | ss. 4(1), 10(b) and 15–20: 1 Dec 1988 ss. 28(b)–(e), 30 and 31: 10 Dec 1991 (see Gazette 1991, No. S332) Remainder: Royal Assent | s. 31(2) |

| Superannuation Legislation (Consequential Amendments and Transitional Provisions) Act 1992 | 94, 1992 | 30 June 1992 | s. 3: 1 July 1990 Remainder: Royal Assent | — |

| Health and Community Services Legislation Amendment Act 1992 | 136, 1992 | 11 Nov 1992 | ss. 38, 39(a), 41, 43, 44(d) and 49: 12 May 1954 (see s. 2(2) and Gazette 1954, p. 1179) s. 40: 1 July 1992 ss. 46 and 47: 18 Dec 1990 Remainder: Royal Assent | s. 24 |

| Health Insurance Commission Amendment Act 1993 | 29, 1993 | 9 June 1993 | 9 June 1993 | — |

| Human Services and Health Legislation Amendment Act 1994 | 80, 1994 | 23 June 1994 | Part 3 (ss. 6–12): 9 June 1993 (g) s. 13: Royal Assent (g) | s. 12 |

| Health Legislation (Powers of Investigation) Amendment Act 1994 | 85, 1994 | 23 June 1994 | 21 July 1994 | s. 2 (rep. by 19, 1996, Sch. 1 [item 1]) |

| as amended by | | | | |

| Health Legislation (Powers of Investigation) Amendment Act 1996 | 19, 1996 | 28 June 1996 | 28 June 1996 | — |

| Health Legislation (Private Health Insurance Reform) Amendment Act 1995 | 41, 1995 | 29 May 1995 | s. 5(2): 1 Oct 1995 (h) | — |

| Health and Other Services (Compensation) (Consequential Amendments) Act 1995 | 132, 1995 | 14 Nov 1995 | 1 Feb 1996 (see s. 2 and Gazette 1996, No. GN2) | — |

| Human Services and Health Legislation Amendment Act (No. 3) 1995 | 149, 1995 | 16 Dec 1995 | Schedule 1 (items 62–68) and Schedule 2 (item 15): Royal Assent (i) | Sch. 1 (item 68)

(rep. by 19, 1996, Sch. 1 [item 2]) |

| as amended by | | | | |

| Health Legislation (Powers of Investigation) Amendment Act 1996 | 19, 1996 | 28 June 1996 | 28 June 1996 | — |

| Statute Law Revision Act 1996 | 43, 1996 | 25 Oct 1996 | Schedule 4 (item 86): Royal Assent (j) | — |

| Health Legislation Amendment (Private Health Insurance Incentives) Act 1997 | 45, 1997 | 22 Apr 1997 | 22 Apr 1997 | — |

| Tax Law Improvement Act 1997 | 121, 1997 | 8 July 1997 | Schedule 3 (item 70): (k) | — |

| Audit (Transitional and Miscellaneous) Amendment Act 1997 | 152, 1997 | 24 Oct 1997 | Schedule 2 (items 805–822): 1 Jan 1998 (see Gazette 1997, GN49) (l) | — |

| Health Insurance Commission (Reform and Separation of Functions) Act 1997 | 159, 1997 | 11 Nov 1997 | Schedule 1 (items 1–34): Royal Assent (m) Schedule 1 (items 39–80): 1 Mar 1998 (see Gazette 1998, No. GN9) (m) Schedule 1 (item 81): 11 Nov 2002 (m) | Sch. 1 (items 31–34, 73–80) |

| Child Care Payments (Consequential Amendments and Transitional Provisions) Act 1997 | 196, 1997 | 8 Dec 1997 | Schedule 1 (item 12): (n) Schedule 1 (items 13–16): (n) | — |

| as repealed by | | | | |

| A New Tax System (Family Assistance) (Consequential and Related Measures) Act (No. 1) 1999 | 82, 1999 | 8 July 1999 | Schedule 2 (item 2): (na) | — |

| Health Legislation Amendment Act 1998 | 19, 1998 | 17 Apr 1998 | Schedule 1 (item 1): Royal Assent (o) | — |

| A New Tax System (Family Assistance) (Consequential and Related Measures) Act (No. 2) 1999 | 83, 1999 | 8 July 1999 | Schedule 8 (items 1–6): 1 July 2000 (p) | — |

| Public Employment (Consequential and Transitional) Amendment Act 1999 | 146, 1999 | 11 Nov 1999 | Schedule 1 (items 509, 510): 5 Dec 1999 (see Gazette 1999, No. S584) (q) | — |

| Corporate Law Economic Reform Program Act 1999 | 156, 1999 | 24 Nov 1999 | Schedule 10 (items 86, 87): 13 Mar 2000 (see Gazette 2000, No. S114) (r) | — |

| Health Legislation Amendment Act (No. 3) 1999 | 159, 1999 | 8 Dec 1999 | Schedule 3 (item 70): 1 Jan 1999 (s) | — |

| as amended by | | | | |

| Health Legislation Amendment Act (No. 2) 2001 | 59, 2001 | 28 June 2001 | Schedule 3 (items 7–10): 15 Dec 1998 (see s. 2(2)) Schedule 3 (item 12): 1 Jan 1999 Remainder: Royal Assent | — |

| Criminal Code Amendment (Theft, Fraud, Bribery and Related Offences) Act 2000 | 137, 2000 | 24 Nov 2000 | Sch 2 (items 220, 221, 418, 419): 24 May 2001 (s 2(3)) | Sch 2 (items 418, 419) |

| Health and Aged Care Legislation Amendment (Application of Criminal Code) Act 2001 | 111, 2001 | 17 Sept 2001 | 17 Sept 2001 | s 4 |

| Abolition of Compulsory Age Retirement (Statutory Officeholders) Act 2001 | 159, 2001 | 1 Oct 2001 | 29 Oct 2001 | Sch 1 (item 97) |

| Health Insurance Commission Amendment Act 2002 | 71, 2002 | 4 Sept 2002 | ss. 1–3 and Schedule 1: Royal Assent Remainder: (t) | Sch 1 (item 4) |

| Medical Indemnity (Consequential Amendments) Act 2002 | 133, 2002 | 19 Dec 2002 | 1 Jan 2003 | — |

| Designs (Consequential Amendments) Act 2003 | 148, 2003 | 17 Dec 2003 | Sch 1 and 2: 17 June 2004 (s 2(1) item 2) | — |

| Medical Indemnity Amendment Act 2004 | 17, 2004 | 23 Mar 2004 | 24 Mar 2004 | — |

| Health and Ageing Legislation Amendment Act 2004 | 50, 2004 | 21 Apr 2004 | Schedule 1 (item 6): Royal Assent | — |

| Medical Indemnity Legislation Amendment (Run- off Cover Indemnity and Other Measures) Act 2004 | 77, 2004 | 23 June 2004 | Schedule 2 (item 2): 1 July 2004 | — |

| Financial Framework Legislation Amendment Act 2005 | 8, 2005 | 22 Feb 2005 | Schedule 2 (items 124, 174): Royal Assent | Sch 2 (item 174) |

Human Services Legislation Amendment Act 2005	111, 2005	6 Sept 2005	Sch 1 and Sch 2): 1 Oct 2005 (s 2(1) items 2–7)	Sch 2 (items 714–719, 721–727, 730, 731) Sch. 2 (item 720) (rep. by 100, 2011, Sch. 1 [item 6])
as amended by				
Statute Stocktake Act (No. 1) 2011	100, 2011	15 Sept 2011	Schedule 1 (item 6): 16 Sept 2011	—
Medical Indemnity Legislation Amendment (Competitive Neutrality) Act 2005	126, 2005	19 Oct 2005	Schedule 1 (item 2): 1 July 2005	—
Health Insurance Amendment (Inappropriate and Prohibited Practices and Other Measures) Act 2007	88, 2007	21 June 2007	Schedule 1: 1 Mar 2008 Remainder: Royal Assent	—
Dental Benefits (Consequential Amendments) Act 2008	42, 2008	25 June 2008	Schedule 1 (items 6–17): 26 June 2008 (see s. 2(1))	—
Health Legislation Amendment (Midwives and Nurse Practitioners) Act 2010	29, 2010	12 Apr 2010	Schedule 2 (items 9–18): 1 July 2010 (see s. 2(1))	—
National Health Amendment (Pharmaceutical Benefits Scheme) Act 2010	126, 2010	23 Nov 2010	Schedule 6 (item 29): 1 Dec 2010	—
Human Services Legislation Amendment Act 2011	32, 2011	25 May 2011	Schedule 1: 1 July 2011	Sch 1 (items 88–99A, 101–116)
Statute Law Revision Act 2012	136, 2012	22 Sept 2012	Schedule 1 (item 68) and Schedule 4 (items 19, 20, 50): 22 Sept 2012 (s 2(1) items 2, 35)	Sch 4 (item 50)
Aged Care (Living Longer Living Better) Act 2013	76, 2013	28 June 2013	Sch 4 (item 11): 1 July 2014 (s 2(1) item 6)	—
Health and Other Legislation Amendment Act 2013	111, 2013	29 June 2013	Sch 1 (items 20- 22): 30 June 2013 (s 2(1) item 4)	—
Norfolk Island Legislation Amendment Act 2015	59, 2015	26 May 2015	Sch 2 (items 223, 224): 1 July 2016 (s 2(1) item 5) Sch 2 (items 356–396): 18 June 2015 (s 2(1) item 6)	Sch 2 (items 356–396)
as amended by				
Territories Legislation Amendment Act 2016	33, 2016	23 Mar 2016	Sch 2: 24 Mar 2016 (s 2(1) item 2)	—
Australian Immunisation Register (Consequential and Transitional Provisions) Act 2015	139, 2015	12 Nov 2015	Sch 1 (item 11): 1 Jan 2016 (s 2(1) item 2)	—
Statute Law Revision Act (No. 1) 2016	4, 2016	11 Feb 2016	Sch 4 (items 1, 186): 10 Mar 2016 (s 2(1) item 6)	—
Statute Update Act 2016	61, 2016	23 Sept 2016	Sch 1 (items 287, 288): 21 Oct 2016 (s 2(1) item 1)	—

(a) The Human Services (Medicare) Act 1973 was amended by section 3 only of the Administrative Changes (Consequential Provisions) Act 1976 , subsection 2(7) of which provides as follows:
(7) The amendments of each other Act specified in the Schedule made by this Act shall be deemed to have come into operation on 22 December 1975.
(b) The Human Services (Medicare) Act 1973 was amended by section 41 only of the Conciliation and Arbitration Amendment Act (No. 2) 1983 , subsection 2(2) of which provides as follows:
(2) Sections 3, 6, 7, 8, 9, 10, 12, 14 and 16, subsection 22(3) and sections 27, 39, 40, 41 and 43 shall come into operation on a date, or respective dates, to be fixed by Proclamation.
(c) The Human Services (Medicare) Act 1973 was amended by subsection 151(1) only of the Public Service Reform Act 1984 , subsection 2(4) of which provides as follows:
(4) The remaining provisions of this Act shall come into operation on such day as is, or such respective days as are, fixed by Proclamation.
(d) The Human Services (Medicare) Act 1973 was amended by section 3 only of the Statute Law (Miscellaneous Provisions) Act (No. 1) 1985 , subsection 2(1) of which provides as follows:
(1) Subject to this section, this Act shall come into operation on the twenty- eighth day after the

day on which it receives the Royal Assent.

(e) The Human Services (Medicare) Act 1973 was amended by Part III (sections 55 and 56) only of the Health Legislation Amendment Act 1986 , subsection 2(1) of which provides as follows:

(1) Section 1, this section, section 3, subsection 19(2), section 23, subsection 47(1), section 53, Part III, section 57, sections 61 to 71 (inclusive) and Parts V and VI shall come into operation on the twenty- eighth day after the day on which this Act receives the Royal Assent.

(f) The Human Services (Medicare) Act 1973 was amended by sections 3–5 only of the Health Legislation (Pharmaceutical Benefits) Amendment Act 1991 , subsection 2(1) and paragraphs (3)(a), (b) and (4)(b) of which provide as follows:

(1) Subject to this section, this Act commences on the day on which it receives the Royal Assent.

(3) The following provisions commence on 1 July 1991:

(a) section 5, paragraph 7(c) and sections 8 and 9;

(b) subsections 8D(1) and (3) inserted in the Health Insurance Commission Act 1973 by section 4 of this Act.

(4) Subject to subsection (5), the following provisions commence on a day (being a day after 1 July 1991) to be fixed by Proclamation:

(b) subsection 8D(2) inserted in the Health Insurance Commission Act 1973 by section 4 of this Act.

(g) The Human Services (Medicare) Act 1973 was amended by Part 3 (sections 6–12) and section 13 only of the Human Services and Health Legislation Amendment Act 1994 , subsections 2(1) and (2) of which provide as follows:

(1) Subject to subsections (2) and (3), this Act commences on the day on which it receives the Royal Assent.

(2) Part 3 is taken to have commenced on 9 June 1993, immediately after the commencement of the Health Insurance Commission Amendment Act 1993 .

(h) The Human Services (Medicare) Act 1973 was amended by subsection 5(2) only of the Health Legislation (Private Health Insurance Reform) Amendment Act 1995 , subsection 2(3) of which provides as follows:

(3) Section 5 and Schedule 2 commence on 1 October 1995.

(i) The Human Services (Medicare) Act 1973 was amended by Schedule 1 (items 62–68) and Schedule 2 (item 15) only of the Human Services and Health Legislation Amendment Act (No. 3) 1995 , subsection 2(1) of which provides as follows:

(1) Subject to this section, this Act commences on the day on which it receives the Royal Assent.

(j) The Human Services (Medicare) Act 1973 was amended by Schedule 4 (item 86) only of the Statute Law Revision Act 1996 , subsection 2(1) of which provides as follows:

(1) Subject to subsections (2) and (3), this Act commences on the day on which it receives the Royal Assent.

(k) The Human Services (Medicare) Act 1973 was amended by Schedule 3 (item 70) only of the Tax Law Improvement Act 1997, subsections 2(2) and (3) of which provide as follows:

(2) Schedule 1 commences on 1 July 1997 immediately after the commencement of the Income Tax Assessment Act 1997 .

(3) Each of the other Schedules (except Schedule 12) commences immediately after the commencement of the immediately preceding Schedule.

(l) The Human Services (Medicare) Act 1973 was amended by Schedule 2 (items 805–822) only of the Audit (Transitional and Miscellaneous) Amendment Act 1997 , subsection 2(2) of which provides as follows:

(2) Schedules 1, 2 and 4 commence on the same day as the Financial Management and Accountability Act 1997 .

(m) The Human Services (Medicare) Act 1973 was amended by Schedule 1 (items 1–34 and 39–81) only of the Health Insurance Commission (Reform and Separation of Functions) Act 1997 , subsections 2(1), (2) and (4) of which provide as follows:

(1) Subject to this section, this Act commences on the day on which it receives the Royal Assent.

(2) Subject to subsection (3), Part 2 of Schedule 1 to this Act commences on the fund- transfer

day.

(4) Part 3 of Schedule 1 to this Act commences at the end of the period of 5 years beginning on the day on which this Act receives the Royal Assent.

(n) The Human Services (Medicare) Act 1973 was amended by Schedule 1 (items 12–16) only of the Child Care Payments (Consequential Amendments and Transitional Provisions) Act 1997 , subsections 2(2) and (4) of which provide as follows:

(2) Subject to subsections (3) to (5), Schedule 1 commences on the day that is the payment commencement day for the purposes of the Child Care Payments Act 1997 .

(4) Item 12 of Schedule 1 commences on the payment commencement day only if item 39 of Schedule 1 to the Health Insurance Commission (Reform and Separation of Functions) Act 1997 has not commenced before that day.

The Child Care Payments (Consequential Amendments and Transitional Provisions) Act 1997 was repealed by Schedule 2 (item 2) of the A New Tax System (Family Assistance) (Consequential and Related Measures) Act (No. 1) 1999 before the amendments made by Schedule 1 (items 13–16) commenced.

The amendment made by Schedule 1 (item 12) did not commence.

(na) The Child Care Payments (Consequential Amendments and Transitional Provisions) Act 1997 was repealed by Schedule 2 (item 2) only of the A New Tax System (Family Assistance) (Consequential and Related Measures) Act (No. 1) 1999 , subsection 2(3) of which provides as follows:

(3) Items 1, 2, 4 and 5 of Schedule 2 commence immediately before the day that is the payment commencement day for the purposes of the Child Care Payments Act 1997 .

The payment commencement day was 19 June 2000.

(o) The Human Services (Medicare) Act 1973 was amended by Schedule 1 (item 1) only of the Health Legislation Amendment Act 1998 , subsection 2(1) of which provides as follows:

(1) Subject to this section, this Act commences on the day on which it receives the Royal Assent.

(p) The Human Services (Medicare) Act 1973 was amended by Schedule 8 (items 1–6) only of the A New Tax System (Family Assistance) (Consequential and Related Measures) Act (No. 2) 1999 , subsection 2(2) of which provides as follows:

(2) Schedule 1 (Parts 1 to 5), Schedules 3 to 6, Schedule 7 (other than item 14), Schedules 8 and 9, Schedule 10 (other than item 63) and Schedule 11 (items 3 and 4 only) commence, or are taken to have commenced, on the commencement of Schedule 1 to the A New Tax System (Family Assistance) (Consequential and Related Measures) Act (No. 1) 1999 .

(q) The Human Services (Medicare) Act 1973 was amended by Schedule 1 (items 509 and 510) only of the Public Employment (Consequential and Transitional) Amendment Act 1999 , subsections 2(1) and (2) of which provide as follows:

(1) In this Act, commencing time means the time when the Public Service Act 1999 commences.

(2) Subject to this section, this Act commences at the commencing time.

(r) The Human Services (Medicare) Act 1973 was amended by Schedule 10 (items 86 and 87) only of the Corporate Law Economic Reform Program Act 1999 , subsection 2(2)(c) of which provides as follows:

(2) The following provisions commence on a day or days to be fixed by Proclamation:

(c) the items in Schedules 10, 11 and 12.

(s) The Human Services (Medicare) Act 1973 was amended by Schedule 3 (item 70) only of the Health Legislation Amendment Act (No. 3) 1999 , subsection 2(5) of which provides as follows:

(5) Schedule 3 is taken to have commenced on 1 January 1999.

(t) Subsection 2(1) (item 3(b)) of the Health Insurance Commission Amendment Act 2002 provides as follows:

(1) Each provision of this Act specified in column 1 of the table commences, or is taken to have commenced, on the day or at the time specified in column 2 of the table.

| Commencement information |
| Column 1 | Column 2 | Column 3 |

| Provision(s) | Commencement | Date/Details |
| 3. Schedule 2 | The later of: (b) immediately after item 81 of Schedule 1 to the Health Insurance Commission (Reform and Separation of Functions) Act 1997 commences | 11 November 2002 |

Endnote 4-Amendment history

Provision affected	How affected
Title	rs. No. 111, 2005
	am. No. 32, 2011
Part I	
s. 1	am. No. 111, 2005; No. 32, 2011
s 3	am No 91, 1976; No 100, 1976; No 134, 1978; No 54, 1983; No 136, 1992; No 80, 1994; No 85, 1994; No 149, 1995; No 159, 1997; No 83, 1999; No 146, 1999; No 71, 2002; No 50, 2004; No 111, 2005; No 88, 2007; No 42, 2008; No 126, 2010; No 32, 2011; No 59, 2015
s. 3A	ad. No. 85, 1994
	am. No. 132, 1995; No. 137, 2000; No. 111, 2001; No. 133, 2002; No. 88, 2007; No. 42, 2008; No. 29, 2010
s 3B	ad No 111, 2001
	rep No 32, 2011
	ad No 59, 2015
Heading to Part II	am. No. 134, 1978
	rs. No. 111, 2005
	rep. No. 32, 2011
Part II	rep. No. 32, 2011
Part IIA	
Heading to Part IIA	ad. No. 111, 2005
	rs. No. 32, 2011
Heading to Div. 1 of Part IIA	ad. No. 111, 2005
	rep. No. 32, 2011
s. 4	rs. No. 111, 2005; No. 32, 2011
s. 4A	ad. No. 111, 2005
	rs. No. 32, 2011
	am. No. 136, 2012
Note to s. 4A(1)	ad. No. 136, 2012
Heading to s. 5	am. No. 111, 2005; No. 32, 2011
Subhead. to s. 5(1)	ad. No. 32, 2011
s. 5	am. No. 100, 1976
	rep. No. 134, 1978
	ad. No. 54, 1983
	rs. No. 159, 1997
	am. No. 111, 2005; No. 32, 2011
Heading to s. 6	am. No. 32, 2011
s. 6	am. No. 100, 1976
	rep. No. 134, 1978
	ad. No. 159, 1997
	rs. No. 111, 2005
	am. No. 32, 2011
Heading to s. 7	am. No. 111, 2005
	rs. No. 32, 2011
s. 7	rep. No. 134, 1978

	ad. No. 159, 1997
	am. No. 111, 2005
	rs. No. 32, 2011
s. 7A	ad. No. 111, 2005
	rs. No. 32, 2011
s. 8	rs. No. 100, 1976
	rep. No. 134, 1978
	ad. No. 159, 1997
	rs. No. 111, 2005
	rep. No. 32, 2011
ss. 8AA, 8AB......................	ad. No. 159, 1997
	rs. No. 111, 2005
	rep. No. 32, 2011
s. 8AC................................	ad. No. 111, 2005
	am. No. 32, 2011
Heading to s. 8AD	am. No. 32, 2011
s. 8AD	ad. No. 111, 2005
	am. No. 32, 2011
Note to s. 8AD(1)	am. No. 32, 2011
Heading to s. 8AE	am. No. 32, 2011
s. 8AE	ad. No. 111, 2005
	am. No. 32, 2011
Note to s. 8AE(1)	am. No. 32, 2011
Heading to s. 8AF	am. No. 32, 2011
s. 8AF	ad. No. 111, 2005
	am. No. 32, 2011
ss. 8AG–8AM	ad. No. 111, 2005
	rep. No. 32, 2011
s. 8A	ad. No. 61, 1976
	rs. No. 100, 1976
	am. No. 134, 1978; No. 54, 1983; No. 41, 1995
	rep. No. 159, 1997
s. 8B	ad. No. 100, 1976
	am. No. 134, 1978; No. 54, 1983
	rep. No. 159, 1997
	ad. No. 32, 2011
Div. 2 of Part IIA	ad. No. 111, 2005
	rep. No. 32, 2011
Part IIA..............................	ad. No. 61, 1976
	rep. No. 100, 1976
Part IIAA	ad. No. 29, 1993
	rep. No. 83, 1999
s. 8BA...............................	ad. No. 29, 1993
	rep. No. 83, 1999
Part IIAB...........................	ad. No. 149, 1995
	rep. No. 159, 1997
s. 8BB	ad. No. 149, 1995
	rep. No. 159, 1997
Part IIAC...........................	ad. No. 149, 1995
	rep. No. 159, 1997
s. 8BC	ad. No. 149, 1995
	rep. No. 159, 1997
Part IIB	ad. No. 134, 1978

	rep. No. 159, 1997
s. 8C	ad. No. 100, 1976
	rs. No. 134, 1978
	am. No. 54, 1983
	rep. No. 159, 1997
s. 8D	ad. No. 100, 1976
	rs. No. 134, 1978
	rep. No. 53, 1979
	ad. No. 119, 1991
	rep. No. 136, 1992
	ad. No. 132, 1995
	rep. No. 159, 1997
s. 8DA	ad. No. 45, 1997
	rep. No. 159, 1997
s. 8E	ad. No. 100, 1976
	am. No. 36, 1978
	rs. No. 134, 1978
	am. No. 54, 1983
	rep. No. 159, 1997
s. 8F	ad. No. 134, 1978
	am. No. 119, 1991
	rep. No. 159, 1997
Heading to Part IIC	am. No. 85, 1994
	rep. No. 111, 2005
Part IIC...............................	ad. No. 134, 1978
	rep. No. 111, 2005
s. 8G	ad. No. 134, 1978
	am. Nos. 152 and 159, 1997
	rep. No. 111, 2005
s. 8H	ad. No. 134, 1978
	am. No. 54, 1983
	rep. No. 111, 2005
s. 8HA	ad. No. 149, 1995
	rep. No. 111, 2005
s. 8J	ad. No. 54, 1983
	am. No. 99, 1988; No. 159, 1997
	rep. No. 111, 2005
s. 8JA................................	ad. No. 159, 1997
	rep. No. 111, 2005
Part IID	
Heading to Part IID	rs. No. 111, 2005; No. 32, 2011
Part IID	ad. No. 85, 1994
Division 1	
s. 8K..................................	ad. No. 85, 1994
ss. 8L, 8M..........................	ad. No. 85, 1994
	am. No. 111, 2005; No. 32, 2011
s. 8N..................................	ad. No. 85, 1994
	am. No. 111, 2001; No. 111, 2005; No. 32, 2011
Division 2	
Heading to s. 8P	am. No. 111, 2005; No. 32, 2011
s. 8P..................................	ad. No. 85, 1994
	am. No. 111, 2005; No. 88, 2007; No. 42, 2008; No. 32, 2011
s. 8Q.................................	ad. No. 85, 1994

	rep. No. 94, 1992
s. 32	rep. No. 111, 2005
Part V	rep. No. 111, 2005
s. 32A...............................	ad. No. 159, 1997
	am. No. 71, 2002
	rep. No. 111, 2005
Heading to s. 33.................	rs. No. 159, 1997
	rep. No. 111, 2005
s. 33	am. No. 36, 1978
	rs. No. 134, 1978
	am. No. 54, 1983; No. 80, 1994; No. 159, 1997; No. 83, 1999; No. 71, 2002
	rep. No. 111, 2005
s. 33A...............................	ad. No. 159, 1997
	rep. No. 71, 2002
Heading to s. 34.................	rs. No. 159, 1997
	rep. No. 71, 2002
s. 34	rs. No. 100, 1976
	rep. No. 134, 1978
	ad. No. 54, 1983
	am. No. 152, 1997
	rep. No. 71, 2002
s. 34AAA	ad. No. 80, 1994
	am. No. 152, 1997
	rep. No. 83, 1999
s. 34A	ad. No. 100, 1976
	am. No. 134, 1978; No. 54, 1983
	rep. No. 159, 1997
ss. 34B, 34C......................	ad. No. 54, 1983
	rs. No. 80, 1994
	rep. No. 159, 1997
s. 35	rs. No. 100, 1976; No. 134, 1978; No. 54, 1983; No. 80, 1994
	am. Nos. 152 and 159, 1997
	rep. No. 159, 1997
s. 36	rs. No. 100, 1976
	am. No. 134, 1978; No. 54, 1983; No. 75, 1986; No. 80, 1994; Nos. 152 and 159, 1997; No. 83, 1999
	rs. No. 71, 2002
	am. No. 8, 2005
	rep. No. 111, 2005
s. 36AA	ad. No. 149, 1995
	am. No. 159, 1997
	rep. No. 71, 2002
s. 36A	ad. No. 100, 1976
	am. No. 36, 1978; No. 54, 1983
	rep. No. 159, 1997
	ad. No. 71, 2002
	rep. No. 111, 2005
s. 37	am. No. 134, 1978; No. 159, 1997
	rep. No. 111, 2005
s. 38	am. No. 100, 1976
	rs. No. 134, 1978
	am. No. 159, 1997; No. 19, 1998; No. 71, 2002
	rep. No. 111, 2005

DISCLAIMER

Printed in Great Britain
by Amazon

19492351R00025